AF438603

This book is dedicated in
loving memory of our father,
Juan Osvaldo Oquendo.
May his passion for books
and creativity live on.

Kindness is Magic

To Levi, 

You are a bright light whose

magic inspires me every day.

Love, Mom

One evening before going to bed,

Levi looked out of his bedroom window,

and gazed up at the stars in the sky.

The stars shined brightly,

like fireflies on a Summer night.

"Mommy," said Levi to his mother,

"why do stars shine so brightly in the sky?"

Levi's mother smiled as she thought
about the wonder and magic that is
in every child's heart.

"Every time we show kindness, a star
shines more brightly in the night sky,"
said his mother.

"How can I show kindness?" asked Levi.

"There are lots of ways to be kind
every day," said his mother.

"You can share and take turns with a friend."

"You can give a friend a compliment,

and use kind words like

 'thank you' and 'please.'"

"Or you can give a friend a hug when they are sad."

Levi thought about what his mother

said, and with great curiosity

he asked,

"why does a star shine brightly

when we are kind

to others?"

"Kindness
has the
power to
make people
feel happy and
that power is magic.
It is the same magic that makes
the stars shine brightly in the night sky.
So every time you look up and admire
the stars, you'll remember all of the
kindness you shared with others and
that you are a part of its magic."

That night, Levi fell asleep thinking of all the ways he would show kindness to others.

List all of the ways that you can show

kindness to others:

1.

2.

3.

4.

5.

About the Author

Karen Oquendo is a mom to an amazing son. She is an educator who is passionate about social emotional awareness in young children. She enjoys spending time with her son and family.

About the Illustrator

Kat Oquendo is a designer, artist and plant lady living in Los Angeles, California. She enjoys traveling, being in nature and spending time with family. To learn more about Kat, please visit her website at katoquendo.com.

www.ingramcontent.com/pod-product-compliance
Lightning Source LLC
Chambersburg PA
CBHW042131110726
48006CB00003B/849